75+
TEAM BUILDING
ACTIVITIES
For REMOTE
TEAMS

SIMPLE WAYS TO BUILD TRUST,
STRENGTHEN COMMUNICATIONS,
AND LAUGH TOGETHER FROM AFAR

CHRISTOPHER
FOUNDER OF BEY
WWW.BEYONDT

D1202434

75+ Team Building Activities for Remote Teams:
Simple Ways to Build Trust, Strengthen Communications,
and Laugh Together from Afar

Cover Design: Christopher Littlefield
Interior Design: Irena Kalcheva
Editors: Betsey Benton and Abby Benton

75+
TEAM BUILDING ACTIVITIES
FOR REMOTE TEAMS

Praise for
75+ Team Building Activities for Remote Teams

"Great practical tips! I love the goodness that Christopher Littlefield puts out into the world. I purchased this wonderful little book and am using many of the tips already. Highly recommend!"

Chester Elton
New York Times bestselling author of
All In and The Carrot Principle

"Managers looking to develop fortified bonds among their teams, Chris has delivered a textbook reference for building an emotional bridge within company culture."

Dorie Clark
Duke & Columbia Business Professor,
author of *Stand Out* and
Top 50 Business Thinker in World -Thinkers50

"Finally a RELIABLE resource for strengthening remote teams."

Ron Carucci
Managing Partner at Navalent and
bestselling author of *Rising to Power*

To Maria and Alia,
thank you for always
keeping life fun and
full of adventure.
I love you more
than the world.

To all the leaders
out there committed to
building cultures
where people
feel valued every day.
Thank you for caring.

Table of Contents

Introduction:

How This Book Will
Make Your Job Easier

I know you have enough on your plate already managing the **work.** I created this book to help you take one thing off your to-do list.

The book is intentionally short: low on reading and high on actions. It is organized in such a way that you can open it five minutes before your meeting to grab a quick game or sit down to plan a longer virtual team retreat. Beyond games, you will find team reflection activities, stay conversation questions, end of the year team reflection exercises, and more. You will also find simple ways to learn, stay healthy, and celebrate together virtually as a team. The only thing you need to do is take action.

How This Book Will Make Your Job Easier
- You will have access to 75+ activity ideas and 100s of questions to help you make your remote meetings, one on ones, and day-to-day virtual interactions more engaging.
- You will have access to downloads, printouts, and other tools to support you.

- Included with the book is a unique link to sign up for the Beyond Thank You Remote Team "Nudge." Every two weeks, for a year, you will receive an email with featured activities from this book, questions and ideas and, when appropriate, Holiday Themed exercises.

This Book Will Not Help You... Decide on which technology to use and why. At this point, each organization tends to have their own preferred platforms for communication. Maybe you use Skype for Business, WebEx, Microsoft Teams, or Zoom. Regardless of what platform you use, all tend to have similar functionalities of video, chat, screen sharing, and most have the ability to separate people into groups. None of the activities in this book require any special technology other than the basic functionalities listed above.

I have spent the last ten years living and running my business from abroad, first from Beirut, Lebanon, and now in Santiago, Chile. The ideas shared in the following pages come from my over 15 years of experience helping companies and leaders across six continents build and maintain cultures where people feel valued and appreciated every day. From both a business and personal level, I understand what it takes to establish and, more importantly, uphold strong relationships with colleagues and family, no matter where they are in the world.

Please feel free to reach out with feedback, questions, or to share your own activity ideas.

Connect via my website
www.beyondthankyou.com

If, after reading this book, you are interested in offering an interactive virtual training or retreat for your team or organization, please check out our programs at:
www.beyondthankyou.com

Team Relationship Building Assessment & Quick Reference

I know you are busy and don't have time to read through all of the 75+ activities in this book. Below is a brief assessment tool and a quick reference section to get you started. For sample meeting and retreat agendas, download the printable Quick Reference Guide from the free bonus sections of the book.

How Are You Really Doing? Use this assessment to reflect on how you're doing at building and maintaining relationships on your team. Without thinking too much, rate your general experience on the following ten questions. After, calculate your total and use the scoring system to see if you need to "Keep it Up," "Step it Up," or "Start it Up." Based on your results, you will find a few recommended activities from the book. If you want to take a step further, think about how you would answer the questions for each member of your team. What do you notice?

Questions	Score
How often do you laugh and play together as a team? 1 Never Often 10	
How often do you do things to learn and grow together? 1 Never Often 10	
How well do you feel you know your team members? 1 Not at All I Know Them Well 10	
If you are feeling burned out, sick, or have a personal issue, how safe do you feel to tell your colleagues? 1 Not Safe at All Completely Safe 10	
If you make a mistake, how comfortable do you feel to admit it to your colleagues? 1 Not Safe at All Completely Safe 10	
If you feel frustrated with a colleague, how comfortable do you feel to ask them to speak? 1 Not Comfortable Completely Comfortable 10	
If you are struggling with a task, how comfortable do you feel to ask for help? 1 Not Comfortable Completely Comfortable 10	
How often do you and your colleagues celebrate and express your appreciation for each other? 1 Never Often 10	
When we have a conflict on the team, we most often... 1 Avoid the Issue Address it Head on 10	
How valued do you feel by your team? 1 Not Valued Fully Valued 10	
Total:	

What is Your Score Telling You?

75+: Keep it Up!*
Keep laughing, learning, and growing together as a team.
Try more challenging activities like:
- Epic Scavenger Hunt
- Difficult Customer Role Play
- What you need to know about working with me!
- Children's Book Challenge
- Year in Review
- Team Shout Outs & Small Victories

*Note - Confirm the feeling is mutual.
Just because you feel this way does not mean everyone else feels
the same. Ask others on your team to take the survey and use the
process as a conversation starter.

50-74: Step it Up!
Time to start injecting a little more fun and reflection into
your work. Don't worry what people will think, just give
something a shot!
Try one of the following activities:
- Pulse Checks Questions
- Question of the Day COVID -19
- Dress Up Day
- Team Shout Outs & Small Victories

As a leader, it's also a good time to schedule one-on-one meetings
with each of your people. Try using the Stay Conversation
questions.

<50: Start it Up!

If this is the case, you have work ahead of you, and you may want to get some additional support. Feel free to reach out to us. Regardless of how overwhelming it may feel, doing nothing to build relationships with your team is probably what got you to where you are right now.

If you want to see a shift, you need to start somewhere. Today, schedule a one-on-one check-in with each of your team members. In this book, you will find a script and list of questions for a

● Stay Conversation.

Time to open the door with your team members and start building emotional safety. In your next meeting, trying to inject a trivia question or question of the day... start small... but start somewhere.

Use the Assessment as Team Reflection Activity: Have each person on your team do the assessment on their own and share their overall results. If there is higher level of openness, have people share the numbers they picked for each question and briefly explain why they choose what they did. After, brainstorm what you could do on an individual level and as a team to further improve your team culture.

Quick Reference

Start Here

Simple activities to get your people talking.

- Team Pulse Check
- Question of the Day
- Question of the Day: COVID-19

Team Rituals

Use these activities every week to nurture a culture of appreciation.

- Small Victories
- Shout Outs

One-to-One Meeting

Make your next conversation more meaningful.

- Stay Conversation

Quick Games

Fun games that take under 10 minutes and require no preparation.

- Home Office Scavenger Hunt
- Orchestra
- Who Am I?
- Name that Tune
- Moving Troll
- Have You Ever (Remote Work Themed!) Word of the Day!
- Two Truths and a Lie

Get to Know You Activities

Help your people learn about each other.

- M & M Question Game
- Whose Cloud Is That?
- My World Your World
- Bring Your Family to Work Day

Take Customer Service to the Next Level

Help your people better understand and serve their clients.

- Know Your Customers Activity
- Difficult Customer Role Play
- Online Customer/Employee Journey Mapping Activity

Great for a Virtual Team Retreat

Use one of these longer activities and host a virtual team retreat.

- Epic Virtual Scavenger Hunt
- Children's Book Challenge
- What You Need to Know About Working with Me
- Year in Review

Free Bonuses

As a thank you for buying this book and to support your commitment to building a great remote team culture, I am offering several free bonus exclusives to my readers. When you purchase this book, you will gain access to copies of the following free handouts and downloads:

75+ Team Building Activities Quick Reference Guide
A printable quick reference of the book. Reminders of the key concepts, sample meeting agendas, and ideas.

Know Your People Form
A form to track all the information you should know about your people.

COVID-19 Resources
Questions to help you understand what your people are facing each day, a list of five things that should be on every virtual meeting agenda, and tips to help your team consciously transition back to work when the time comes!

One Year Subscription to the Beyond Thank You Remote Team "Nudge"
Sadly, like remote employees, books can fall into the trap of out of sight, out of mind. You buy the book in a moment of clarity,

scroll through a few pages, get inspired to take action, then life happens, and you get distracted. When you download the free bonus, you will have the opportunity to sign up for the Beyond Thank You Remote Team "Nudge." Every two weeks, I will send out activities, meeting prompts, and other ideas from this book directly to your email – a little nudge to remind you to take action. If these are unhelpful, you can unsubscribe any time.

The free downloads are available at the below address:
www.beyondthankyou.com/75-team-building-book-download

The Heart of the Matter

According to research firm Gallup, 70% of the variance in an employee's level of engagement is dependent upon their relationship with their managers.[1] When it comes to developing and maintaining a strong foundation, we need to keep the following in mind:

Know Your People

If you have ever had someone remember a small detail you shared about yourself in the past, you know how good it makes you feel. One of the simplest ways to show we care is to take time to know our people. Although not everyone is interested in sharing about their personal life (it's important to respect that), most people appreciate when you take time to learn about their lives and interests in and outside of work. In the free downloads provided, you will find the **Know Your People** handout with a list of basic things you should know about your people. Information like preferred name, nicknames, role, spouse/partner name, kids' names, birthday, holidays observed, and more. It also encourages you to learn about their favorite

---

1. Randall Beck and Jim Harter, "Managers Account for 70% of Variance in Employee Engagement," Gallup - Business Journal, last modified April 21, 2015, https://news.gallup.com/businessjournal/182792/managers-account-variance-employee-engagement.aspx.

local restaurant, snacks/sweets they enjoy most, and hobbies outside of work. (More on why this is important below.) This is a great list of things to ask when onboarding a new hire or to use later in a one-on-one or virtual meeting.

Beyond the basic personal information, great leaders keep a pulse on the following of their people:

- Current projects and workloads (from you and from others, if that is the case)
- Current challenges/barriers (at home or work, if they share)
- Skills they are working on developing
- Upcoming events they may have – Major Presentations, Vacations, Weddings, Graduations, Surgeries, etc.

Know Your People's Culture

Do you work with people from other cultures or based in a different part of the world? Show people you value them by valuing their culture.

Here are a few things to keep in mind

The best way to learn about cultural differences is by taking the time to ask questions. Here are a few to try:

- What do you wish people in my culture/country understood about working with yours?
- What are the silly mistakes foreigners often make when visiting/working in your country?
- If you moved, what would you miss the most about your culture/country?
- If I was going to come and visit, what advice would you give me?

Do your research and be aware of local holidays and cultures. Put them in your calendar. Don't assume they observe the holidays, but also don't assume they don't! Stay present to where your employees are. Check the BBC World News app from time to time and watch for major event stories. It means a lot to people when you show you are aware and care about where they are.

Be Inclusive: Care that they're there

Oftentimes, remote employees or quiet employees often get forgotten in virtual meetings. As a leader, show people you care they are there by always including them in the invite, checking in when they are not on the call, and asking for their input when they are attending. If you have a more introverted employee that may be hesitant to speak up, ask by name for their input: "John, we have been talking a lot, what is your thought on X?" and then give them time to respond, to signal you value their input.

Beyond meeting, make sure you include people by...

- Making them aware of organizational town halls and company-wide events and finding ways to have them participate remotely.
- Sharing training opportunities.
- Including them if employees are meeting locally after work. Give them a call or send them a picture.
- Inviting them, even if they can't physically make it, to a birthday party, celebration, or team event. Let them know they will be missed.

Tip: Do you have a hard time remembering to include your remote employees? Keep a photo of your team member on your desktop or at your workspace. Each time you are about to send an invite, get in the habit of checking to make sure that everyone who should be invited, is.

Be Considerate: Respect their Time, Time Zone, & Lives Outside of Work

One of the simplest and often overlooked ways to show remote employees you value them is by valuing their time. Leaders often unintentionally burn bridges when they send emails in the middle of the night or messages on weekends. They may be available 24 hours a day, but that does not mean their people are. Leaders who respect the time and personal lives of their people often win their trust and regard. This starts by taking time to understand the lives and commitments of their people. Do your employees have kids, siblings, or elderly parents that they are responsible for caring for? Are your employees in university, taking classes, or working additional jobs to supplement their income? When you take time to understand their lives outside of work, you are better equipped to support them at work.

Here are some additional ways to be considerate of people's time:

- Do your employees work in a different time zone? Every once in a while, schedule a meeting in their working hours, not just yours. Waking up in the middle of the night from time to time so they don't have to sends a powerful message that you care for their wellbeing.
- Are your employees working parents or students? Take a few minutes to understand their needs and see what you can do to try and schedule in a way that makes their lives easier.
- Avoid sending work emails, Slack messages, WhatsApps, or anything else during their time off. Before hitting send, always ask, "Do I need to send this right now?" It may take something off your to-do list, but it just added it to theirs at 2 A.M.

COVID-19: During the current health crisis, check in regularly and be as flexible as possible while you and your people adapt to a new work environment and schedule. Everyone is facing the same crisis, but not facing the same circumstances.

Be Grateful: Let people know you value their contribution.
A few years back, I heard Chester Elton, the author of the book, Leading with Gratitude, share the following: "How long does it take for a manager to connect with a remote employee who has done something wrong? About a minute. How long does it take for that manager to connect with a remote employee who has done something right? Maybe never." Regardless if the person is in the same room or working from home, people need to know that what they do is appreciated.

Here are a few simple ways to show people you are grateful for their contributions:
- When people join a virtual meeting, let them know you appreciate them being there. During the health crisis, add that you appreciate them still working with all the uncertainty and additional responsibilities they now have.
- When people submit deliverables, acknowledge you received them and offer feedback. If you use their work, give them credit. If you don't use their work, take five minutes to let them know why.
- Show people you are grateful for their contributions by giving them time to share in a meeting or one to one.
- When they do exceptional work, share it with senior leaders.
- For more tips on giving a compliment, please check out my article in Harvard Business Review, "How to Give and Receive Compliments at Work." https://hbr.org/2019/10/how-to-give-and-receive-compliments-at-work

Be Available: Let them know you are there for them

For the last two years, I conducted all the qualitative interviews for a best place to work study. In my interviews with the CEOs of the top ten places to work in this field, there was one thing that was apparent, all of them made themselves available to employees from every level. Whether through monthly town halls, virtual office hours, lunches, or going for coffee, these leaders understood that one of the most valuable things they could offer their people was their time and support. In order to engage people, you need to engage with them. This starts by showing our people we are here to support them.

How to show people you are available:

- Let your people know the best times to reach you and the best ways to reach you. (Email, WhatsApp, Slack, etc.)
- Interview your people about what amount of communication works best for them.
- Do a small virtual check in each day.
  - "Hey, I'm online if you have any questions."
  - "How is your project going today?"
  - "I'll be online after 3 p.m. today if you need anything."

Be a People Developer – Help Your People Grow

Show people you value them by valuing their technical and career development. This starts by investing time in one on ones to ask about personal and professional goals, then finding ways to support them in accomplishing those goals.

How to support people's development

- Provide regular feedback on their work and give them time to ask questions.
- When they make a mistake, help them understand why and work together to get it right.
- Share articles and resources related to further developing their technical expertise.
- Create stretch assignments.
- Let them know about trainings, job postings, and other opportunities.
- Help them connect with other internal and external people in your field.
- Work with them to craft their job to help meet their goals.

Boosting the Remote Relationship

Research by Joseph Grenny and his company Vital Smarts,[2] found that "virtual teammates are 2.5 times more likely to perceive mistrust, incompetence, broken commitments, and bad decision making with distant colleagues than those who are co-located. Worse, they report taking 5 to 10 times longer to address their concerns." Grenny goes on to share that in order to address this issue, the key is creating Safety. "When people feel safe, they open up. When they don't, they shut down. People only feel safe enough to venture into dicey dialogue when those around them generate sufficient positive evidence of their intentions and respect."

Regardless, if you are a senior leader, middle manager, or individual contributor, if we want to create a remote team culture where great work gets done, it starts with investing in building and maintaining strong relationships with your team.

In Order to Engage Remote Employees,
You Must Engage with Them

2. Joseph Grenny, "How to Raise Sensitive Issues During a Virtual Meeting," Harvard Business Review, last modified March 14, 2017, https://hbr.org/2017/03/how-to-raise-sensitive-issues-during-a-virtual-meeting.

Our Physical Proximity often provides the small positive social interactions that bolster our relationships. Working remotely, we cannot depend on unplanned run-ins, so instead, we must intentionally build them into our virtual interactions.

When working remotely, our interactions tend to consist of:

- Virtual team meetings
- One on one's
- Phone calls
- Chats
- Texts
- Email communications

And, if you are connected to your team members via social media (Facebook, Instagram, Twitter, LinkedIn, etc.), social media posts and comments.

Just because we are not in the same location does not mean we can't have a physical impact. Below are a few simple ways to be present from afar.

Have Physical Presence without Being There

Establish an Internal Partner

Reach out to a fellow manager or staff member at the location of your remote team member (if they work at home this may be a family member). Use this person to help you collect intel on what your employee likes/dislikes, and to help you surprise them from time to time by dropping things off for you.

Food

Is your team working late putting in extra hours? Did they just finish a big project? Surprise them by having food delivered!

A quick search on Yelp/TripAdvisor and you will find a list of the best delivery places near their office.

Coffee

Do you have a remote one on one with an employee? Take them out to lunch from afar or buy them a cup of coffee. Ask them where they are going to go, make a quick call to the coffee shop, and prepay for their meal or drink ahead of time. If you can't do that, send a gift card to use when you are meeting.

Flowers for Family

Send flowers/food to the family of your employee to thank them for supporting your employee during busy times. I guarantee they will never forget the gesture!

Happy Birthday/Work Anniversary/Promotion

Have a cake made by a local bakery and, in addition to the standard message, ask them to write "from" ... and list all the team members' names on the cake.

Send a Book

Is your employee interested in a certain topic? Send them a book, article, or magazine subscription you think they will love.

Do they have Kids?

Send a children's book you loved as a kid to them. (When my daughter was born, a client in Australia sent me three children's books to my home in Chile! My daughter reads them daily and I think of my client every time! Thank You, Amanda Moroney, for the idea.)

*Note: All of these recommendations need to be in parallel with setting clear objectives, holding people accountable, delegating responsibility, and continuously driving key business results. **If you are not doing the above, none of the actions below will make a difference.***

"If we are not building relationships, they are breaking down."

- Guy Maytal, M.D.
Chief of Integrated Care and Pyscho-Oncology
at Weill Cornell Medicine

4 Rules for Successful Activities

Rule 1: Always Start with Connection before Content

Have you ever had someone walk up to you and ask for something without even saying hello? It can feel extremely awkward, if not rude. It's important to start every meeting or call by taking a minute to first connect before jumping into content. Maybe it's a quick check in – "How are you doing?" – or an icebreaker game. A good rule of thumb is to spend the first 5 minutes of your interactions to connect before going into content. (*A big thanks to the amazing Chad Littlefield and Will Wise of We and Me, Inc. for the concept of "Connection and Content". Check out their amazing work at weand.me.*)

Rule 2: The "One Sixth Rule" for Virtual Meetings

In general, it's important to always maintain balance between talking about the actual work, and building and maintaining the relationships that support us to do so. I recommend that for every hour of meeting, ten minutes is devoted to relationship building. This does not mean you always spend 10 minutes playing games. It means that you devote ten minutes throughout your one hour to connect, check in, reflect, learn, laugh, and celebrate. Maybe you spend five minutes in the beginning of the call for check-ins and five minutes at the end of the call to give shout outs.

If you have a 2-hour meeting, give people a stretch break or play a quick game. If you have a 3-hour virtual meeting, you need to step back and ask yourself, "why?" That makes no sense.

Rule 3: Always have Variety & Surprise

How many times have you come to a virtual meeting prepared to work on something else? The whole purpose of creating this book is to give you simple ways to inject a little variety and fun into your remote interactions. Keep your people tuned in and on their toes by surprising them with a mix of activities. Consciously curate the virtual interactions of your team by injecting a mix of questions, games, reflection, learning, and surprises.

Rule 4: Consistency and Ritual

Although it may seem contradictory to the above, it's also important to create consistent team practices and rituals. When people know you will begin every meeting by asking if anyone wants to give a shout out to a coworker, share a recent success, or ask for help, they will come prepared to answer. If every six weeks people have a one on one with their boss, a team debrief session, or a reflection process, they know when they will have a time to speak up, share, and celebrate.

Virtual Facilitation Tips

Here are a few tips to help in facilitating your remote team activities:

Manage Time
If you scheduled 10 minutes for an activity, it's important that you honor that. If you're noticing time is running out and not everyone has participated, that's ok, you can do a few things to move forward:

- Ask the group if they want to keep going for 5 more minutes, but also request people to be brief in their responses.
- Call the activity and pick up where you left off in your next meeting.
- Or, just stop the activity after the allotted time.

Model How You Want People to Participate
After you have introduced an activity, model how you want people to participate. If you ask a question, start by answering it yourself. If you want people to be brief, model a brief answer. If you want people to give more detail, then model sharing more. People tend to model the response of the first person to go.

Have People Prepare Ahead of Time

If you are facilitating a longer activity that requires people to reflect on a question or do prep work, save time by sending the information to them in advance. Before you start the activity, give people 2 minutes to review their notes. (This will also give the people who did not prepare, time to do the work as well.)

Keep the Conversation Moving

It's hard enough to get people to share in regular meetings, let alone remote ones. If people do not immediately respond, call on them by name. "Kevin, what is your answer?" Usually, after a few people go, others tend to warm up and start jumping in on their own. If there is a lull, call on someone else or wrap up the activity. Always keep the conversation moving.

Dealing with Mr. or Mrs. Talks-a-lot!

If you have a person that always jumps in and dominates the conversation, there are a few things you can do. One, set ground rules for your virtual meetings and activities such as, "Give others an opportunity to share before speaking again." Or, "Keep responses to one minute or less." This way, when the person jumps in again, you can say, "John, before you share again, let's hear from some other people." If it's a constant problem, talk to the person on the side and make them aware. In my experience, Mr. Talks-a-lots are often not aware of how they dominate the airspace.

The Bowl of Names

Keep a bowl or bag on your desk with all your team members' names on little slips of paper. Use the bag to randomly choose a person to answer questions, go first in activities, etc. After, take the name out of the bowl until you have worked through everyone and then put them back in and start again. This way, everyone will get picked at one point.

Share the Facilitation Responsibilities

Have everyone take on responsibility for keeping your interactions fun and engaging. Invite other people to choose and facilitate activities in future meetings. If you know about your meetings in advance, assign people to run an activity or discussion for each one.

Get to Know Each Other

Question of the Day

Time: 10 Minutes (or less)
Group: Up to 15
Logistics & Supplies: None

Help your people get to know each other better by jumpstarting each one of your meetings with a question of the day. Pick one of the questions below or choose another from the questions section in the back of the book. Is your whole team in the same Chat or WhatsApp group? Try posting a question of the day or week there as well.

Get to Know You Questions:
- If you could click a button and one task on your to-do list would be automatically completed, what would it be and why?
- What was your favorite dish as a child?
- What made you smile in the last week?
- What is one thing you learned recently that really surprised you?
- What is the most beautiful thing/place you have ever seen and why?
- What simple things give you the most joy?
- What is one of your proudest moments?
- If you could only watch one genre of movie, what would it be and why?
- Tell me of a stranger who impacted your life.
- What do you do to relax?
- What is the strangest job you have ever had?
- What is your motto in life?

- Who was your favorite teacher in school and why?
- What is your favorite quote?
- What movie have you watched more than 5 times?
- What was your favorite toy as a child?
- What grosses you out?
- What is the food you eat most when you're stressed?
- What is the strangest thing you have ever eaten?
- Where is the last place you went on vacation?
- Do you play any instruments? If so, what?
- When you were a kid, what did you think you would do when you grew up?

Question of the Day: COVID-19

Questions:

- What did you used to take for granted, but really appreciate now?
- What is the silver lining in all of this for you?
- What has been the most challenging part of having to work remotely?
- What is your daily routine?
- What have you been doing to take care of yourself?

My World Your World

Time: 10 Minutes (or less)
Group: Up to 15
Logistics & Supplies: Email instructions ahead of activity

Help people better understand each other's worlds outside of work. Have everyone create one PowerPoint slide with pictures from their everyday life using two to three ideas from the list below. Do this with everyone occasionally on Slack, in your meetings, or via email. This is especially a great activity to do when people live in different regions or countries.

- Picture of what inspires you in life
- Picture of who you admire most in the world, alive or dead
- Picture of your home
- Picture from your drive to work (what traffic looks like!)
- Picture of your office
- Picture of where you like to work when not in the office
- Picture of where you typically go to lunch
- Picture of your family
- Picture of your favorite place to go in your City
- Picture of your University
- Picture of your favorite movie characters
- Picture of you as a baby, toddler, teen, university student
- Worst School Picture or Wackiest Childhood Outfit contest

Bring Your Family to Work Day

Time: 10 Minutes (or less)

Group: Up to 15

Logistics & Supplies: Video on

Email invitation ahead of activity

Whether your people work from home, or not, set up a time to meet each other's families. Sometimes this will happen organically as a child busts through the door but, if not, create an opportunity for team members to introduce each other to their family and friends. Please note, in some cultures this is extremely important, and, for others, they may want to keep their work and personal life separate. Propose the ideas and make it an option for those who are interested. Also, remember that pets are invited too!

Tip: If people don't live with their family, have them join via video.

Local Tour

Time: 10 Minutes (or less)
Group: Up to 15
Logistics & Supplies: Video on
Email instructions ahead of activity

Whether it's a tour of their home office or their stomping grounds, give people an opportunity to show others around their local areas. In most places in the world, the cell network is strong enough to connect to video while walking down the street. Ask someone on your team to walk you around the block, show you their local coffee shop, and even introduce you to the people they bump into every day. Do you all live in the same city, but in different areas? Have people share their favorite part of the area they live in – their favorite restaurant, store, park, etc. Give your people a window into each other's world.

Tip: If you are the leader of the group, start by offering to give people a tour of your area. When you do it, it will give others the ok to do the same.

Tip: If people are stuck at home, have them give a tour of their apartment or share the view from their balcony.

Tip: Remember, not everyone may want to share their physical space. Give people the opportunity to opt out.

M & M Question Game

Time: 10 Minutes (or less)
Group: Up to 15
Logistics & Supplies: Video on
M&Ms (or virtual die)
Questions

Have everyone on your team buy a bag of M&Ms before your next meeting. Or, even better, send them a bag! Everyone holds their bag up to the screen, picks out one M&M, and shows the group the color (this way they can't cheat), and answers the corresponding question.

Red: What was one of your most embarrassing moments at work?
Orange: What is one of your proudest moments at work?
Yellow: What made you laugh in the last week?
Green: Where is your favorite place to be outside?
Blue: If you could go anywhere in the world today, where would you go?
Brown: What do you do to ground yourself when you're frustrated?

Tip: Replace the questions with trivia areas. Red: Workplace Safety Questions, Blue: Policy Questions, Yellow: Client Information, etc.

Tip: Don't have M&Ms? Use numbers instead of colors and have one person role a die to select the questions.

Whose Cloud Is That?

Time: 10 Minutes (preparation - 1 Hour)
Group: Up to 15
Logistics & Supplies: Preparation – Survey team members & create word clouds

Guess the Team Member Word Cloud (taken from the book 15 Commitments of Conscious Leaders[3]).Make a short online survey (Survey Monkey works great) with each team member's name and a text box below. Have everyone on the team take the survey and write 3-5 words to describe each person. After, use the words written about each team member in the survey to make a word cloud for them. Share the word cloud in your next virtual meeting via screen share and have people try and guess who each cloud represents. After, send people their word clouds. Word Cloud Generator: https://www.wordclouds.com

---

3. Jim Dethmer, Diana Chapman, and Kaley Klemp, *The 15 commitments of conscious leadership: a new paradigm for sustainable success* (United States: Conscious Leadership Group, 2015).

Remote Office Tour & Best Practices Share

Time: 10 Minutes (or less)
Group: Up to 15
Logistics & Supplies: Video on

Invite people to give each other a tour of their remote office set up. Ask for a volunteer or pick someone to explain their set up, their work routine, what works well for them, and what doesn't. Use this to jumpstart a conversation about how to best support each other in working remotely.

Letter from the Crisis

Time: 10 Minutes (or less)
Group: Up to 15
Logistics & Supplies: None

Have everyone on your team write a letter to themselves from the crisis. Have them share their reflections about how they are feeling, what it has been like for them, and how they think this whole situation will impact them, and the world, moving forward. After, have them seal up their letter or send them the note via email. One year from now, ask people to open their letter and read what they wrote!

Check Ins & Debriefs

High and Low

Time: 10 Minutes (or less)
Group: Up to 15
Logistics & Supplies: None

This is a great quick check-in or debrief question to use after a tough week, a major project or event finishes, or at the end of a long meeting. Go around and ask everyone to share one high (favorite moment/accomplishment) and one low (least favorite moment/frustration). Ask people...

What was your high and low...
- from today's meeting?
- from this past week?
- since we last spoke?
- on this project?

Example: *"My high today was finally finishing the report I have been working on for months. My low, I accidently missed a meeting with a client today."*

Tip: Make it a ritual – ask this question at the end of each weekly meeting. After a while, people will come ready to answer the questions.

Tip: As the activity leader, the first few times you ask the questions, model answering the questions first. If you keep your answer succinct, so will they!

Team Pulse Check

Time: 10 Minutes (or less)
Group: Up to 15
Logistics & Supplies: Pulse check questions

Do you ever struggle to get your people to open up and talk in meetings? It's hard enough to get people to open up in person, let alone remotely, on a video or phone conference. How do we build connection and check in with our people when they don't talk or share?

Remember as a teenager when an authority figure asked, "*How are you doing?*" Without thinking, the answer was always "*Ok*" or "*Fine*" even when that wasn't true. This was because we sometimes didn't want to talk about how we were really feeling, were not sure it was safe to talk about it, or because we didn't know how to talk about it.

As adults, we generally have a better idea of how to express our feelings and concerns, but still need help sometimes talking and sharing with our mentors, coworkers, and friends.

Working with groups for the last fifteen years, one of my favorite practices to support sharing is by using **Pulse Check Questions:** *Asking people both to reflect on and express how they feel through a number.*

In your next virtual meeting, instead of asking people how they are doing, try the following:

1. Ask people to open the chat window and type the number that best represents their response to one of questions below:

Energy Level: What is your energy level right now, from 1-completely drained, to 10-fully charged?

Support at Work: How supported do you feel right now at work, from 1-not supported at all, to 10-fully supported?

Support at Home: How supported do you feel right now at home, from 1-not supported at all, to 10-fully supported?

Communication Effectiveness: How do you feel we are communicating on our team, from 1-not communicating well at all, to 10-communicating clearly, efficiently, and at our best?

Feeling Valued: How valued do you feel right now at work, from 1-not valued at all, to 10-extremely valued?

Inclusion: How included do you feel on this team, from 1-not included at all, to 10-fully included?

2. Let everyone have a few moments to write their number. **Tip:** As a leader, model openness. If you are feeling burned out, put a low number to let others know they can as well.

3. Follow up by asking if anyone wants to share why they chose the number they did and if there is anything you or the team could do to help move that number up. **Note:** Do not force people to share, not everyone feels safe to share publicly.

4. As a leader, take note if anyone writes a number lower than 7. Use this as a signal to reach out and check in. *"Hey Kevin, I noticed that you shared you were feeling a bit burned out. I wanted to follow up and see if there is anything I can do to support you."*

Stay Conversation

Time: 30 Min—1 Hour
Group: One-to-One
Logistics & Supplies: Stay conversation questions

Most people have heard of the idea of an exit interview where you interview an employee about why they have decided to leave the company. All too often, the reason they are leaving could have been avoided if we had just taken the time to check in prior. A "Stay Conversation" is a simple check in with your employee every 2-3 months to see how things are going and if there is anything you can do to better support them.

Context: Remember, this is not a performance review, but an intentional check in to see how the employee's experience is going. Your job is to listen and understand their experience and identify ways to better support them.

Introduction:
I just wanted to check in and see how things have been going for you. I really appreciate having you on our team and I wanted to make sure you're having a good experience.

Possible Stay Conversation Questions
- In general, how have things been going?
- What part of your job do you enjoy the most? The least?
- What has been your biggest challenge? How can I better support you with that challenge?
- Is there any feedback you would give to me on how to better support you overall?

- If there anything you want feedback from me on?
- Do you feel like you are learning and growing here? If no, what do you want to be learning? How can I help facilitate?
- Do you feel like you are getting opportunities to work on the kind of projects you want to be working on?
- Is there anything I can do to help improve your experience here?
- What do you want to be acknowledged for?
- What job related goals would you like to accomplish in the next 6 (12) months?

After, commit to follow up actions and a next meeting.

What You Need to Know About Working with Me Conversation

Time: 1.5—2 Hours
Group: Up to 10
Logistics & Supplies: Working with Me questions

This is a great activity to help your team become more aware of how people work at their best, how to spot frustration, and how to better support one another working remotely. Inform your team that in the next meeting you want to devote time to better understand how each other works at their best. Send everyone the below questions, ask them to write down their answers ahead of time, and come to the next meeting ready to share.

Start off your meeting by introducing the activity & ground rules

Hi Everyone, we spend a lot of time working together but not much time talking about how we work together. Today, I wanted to spend our call learning to better understand each other and how we work. Each person will have 1-3 minutes to share their responses to the questions. After, people can ask clarifying questions to better understand what the person shared, but it's not a time to challenge or make them feel wrong. Would anyone like to volunteer to go first?

As the Activity Facilitator, give each person 1-3 uninterrupted minutes to share their answers to the question. After, ask people if they have any clarifying questions. Note - Some people may try to do some discrete jabs at a person... if you question someone's intention, just ask "Are you clarifying something they said or

are you judging what they said? Please honor our ground rules."
After people ask questions, move to the next person.

Possible Questions: (Pick 3-5)
This is how I explain what I do to others outside of work:
- I spend the majority of my time each day...
- The hardest part of my job is...
- What I wish people understood about what it takes to do my job (maybe given my other responsibilities) is...
- The people I work best with understand the following about me...
- My problem-solving process is ...
- Some of the signs that I am frustrated or becoming frustrated are... (phone, email, in person) (What does it look and sound like?)
- The best way to support me when I am frustrated is...
- The behaviors, actions, and attitudes at work that have me feeling most valued are...
- What I am most proud of is...
- What I love about my work and my team is...

Possible Closing:
Thank you everyone for your openness and willingness to share. It's taking time to better understand each other that helps us work better together as a team.

Tip: Unless you have several hours, you may not have time for everyone to do this in one meeting. Try doing one per meeting over several weeks.

Tip: This is a great activity to get to know a new team member or help them understand others.

Year in Review

Time: 1.5-2 Hours

Group: Up to 15

Logistics & Supplies: Send individual reflection questions ahead of time

Team reflection questions

Here is an opportunity to mix it up and offer your people something truly unique that will have a lasting impact on your organization's culture and performance. This year, guide your team through a simple and fun year-in-review process.

Instructions

1. Pick a date, time for your event, and invite your team.

2. Email each team member with a copy of the Individual Reflection Questions.

3. Set the tone for the session by introducing the purpose of the activity and the process.

4. Present each of the below questions to the group. Give participants a few minutes to personally reflect after each one, then open the floor for people to share. Make it clear from the start (especially for the personal questions) that no one is required to share if they don't want to. As people share, capture key lessons and accomplishments for your team in a shared document.

5. Afterwards, go through the shared list together and celebrate the amazing wealth of growth and learning! Follow up with a virtual drink together!

Introduction & Purpose:

"Today we are going to take a few hours to stop and reflect back on our last year. Most of the time, we get so busy at work that it's hard to remember what happened yesterday, let alone what happened twelve months ago. When we get busy, we tend quickly to shift from project to project often passing over key accomplishments, insights, and lessons. Today is about taking the time to really get present and celebrate how much we have grown individually and as a team over the last year."

Team Reflection questions

What major events/changes/challenges did we face in our organization over the last year?

- What skills or abilities have we developed or further developed as a team in the past year?
- What were some of the major challenges at work? What did you do to overcome them?
- What lessons have you learned personally?
- What lessons have we learned as a team?
- How have we grown as a team this year?
- What are you most proud of our team for?
- As part of this team, what are you most grateful for looking back on this year?

Individual Reflection Questions

Take a few minutes to stop and reflect on the last 12 months. Use the questions below to reflect on and celebrate your ongoing growth and development. (Note: This is just for your personal reflection, not the team.)

- What were my favorite moments and unique experiences over the last year?

- What were the work challenges and barriers I faced (or am still facing)?
- What were the personal challenges and barriers I faced (or am still facing)?
- What were my major accomplishments?
- What new skills did I develop (or improve)?
- What am I most proud of from the last year?
- What did I learn about myself and how I work over the last year?
- What am I most proud of?

Laugh & Play Together

Word of the Day!

Time: 10 Minutes (or less)
Group: Up to 15
Logistics & Supplies: None

At the start of each meeting, pick a word of the day, such as "cucumber". See who can slip the word into the conversation without others noticing. "I really think that if we cucumber the system with a little extra investment, everything will work much faster." If you catch someone using the word, yell "word of the day!"

Home Office Scavenger Hunt

Time: 10 Minutes (or less)
Group: Up to 15
Logistics & Supplies: Video on
List of scavenger hunt items

If all your people are working from home, organize a rapid-fire home office scavenger hunt. Come up with a list of 5-8 items, using the list below for ideas. Tell everyone you are about to run a home scavenger hunt. You will mention an item and see who can get back to their computer with it the fastest. Reward one point for having an item and a bonus point for getting back first.

Possible Items:
- Rosemary
- Piece of athletic equipment
- T-shirt of a band/from a concert
- Baby picture
- Old piece of tech (phone, Walkman, etc.)
- Square of toilet paper
- An expired item of food from your pantry (bonus to the person with the most expired item)
- Money from another country
- Your favorite book

Tip: One Item Scavenger Hunt: Do a quick version by asking people to only find one item. If this is the case, it's best to pick something that will spark conversation and sharing like baby picture or a T-shirt from a concert or event attended. After, ask people to do a one-minute explanation of the item and the story behind it.

Have You Ever (Remote Work Themed!)

Time: 10 Minutes (or less)

Group: Up to 15

Logistics & Supplies: "Have You Ever" prompts

With a few tweaks, this typical slumber party game can be a great way to trigger laughs on your virtual team. If you have never played Have You Ever, it's pretty simple. One person asks a question to the group, for example, *"Have you ever faked a bad connection to get off a conference call?"*

Everyone who has done that thing has to hold up their hand in front of the camera!

It is best if you have people create their own questions, but here are a few to get you started:

Have you ever...

- Gone to the bathroom while on a call?
- Stopped paying attention then got asked a question and faked your answer?
- Really not had pants on?
- Piled things under your desk and out of sight to look like your office was cleaner than it was?
- Forgotten a call completely until the host called you?
- Fallen asleep while others were talking?
- Watched a full show on YouTube or Netflix while on a call?
- Lied about having a bad signal to justify not using video because you were somewhere you were not supposed to be?
- Done laundry or cooked a meal while on a call?

Tip: If your platform allows you to turn cameras off and on easily, make this more visual by having people turn off their cameras, and then turn them back on if they have done that thing!

Moving Troll

Time: 10 Minutes (or less)
Group: Up to 15
Logistics & Supplies: Video on
                             None

Have everyone on your team pick an object like a little troll or book they have in their office. Before each call, have people move the object to a different location within the camera's view. See who can spot the change. Another version is to have people turn off their cameras for 30 seconds and change one thing in their office. After, ask people to guess what change was made!

Who Am I?

Time: 10 Minutes (or less)
Group: Up to 15
Logistics & Supplies: None

This is a quick game to bring a little fun and play to your next virtual meeting. Have one team member pick a famous person, alive or dead. Next, have others ask the yes or no questions until they have enough information to guess who they are.

Are you alive? No

Are you a musician? Yes

Did you die in the last 10 years? Yes

Are you a man? Yes

Are you a Country singer? No

Rock singer? Yes

Are you a solo artist? Yes

Are you? Prince

YES!

Freeze

Time: 10 Minutes (or less)
Group: Up to 15
Logistics & Supplies: Video on
                            None

It is hard to have a video call without someone's screen freezing in an awkward position. Turn this sad reality into a game by trying to fool each other into thinking you're frozen. Stop mid-sentence in an awkward position and hold it. If someone says "Looks like John is frozen" – that is a point for you! Did your coworker's screen freeze in an awkward position? Take a screen capture or a photo and keep a collection of Best Awkward Freezes!

Tuned In

Time: 10 Minutes (or less)
Group: Up to 15
Logistics & Supplies: Video on
                                      None

Have everyone write "Tuned In" on a piece of paper. When you feel like people are not paying attention, hold the "Tuned In" sign up to your web cam. Last person to get their sign up is "it" and must either answer a question about his or her self or complete another challenge of your choosing! Not only will it increase meeting attention, but laughs as well!

Last to the Call

Time: 10 Minutes (or less)
Group: Up to 15
Logistics & Supplies: None

Do you have a hard time getting people to show up on time to your calls? If the reason is not because of other responsibilities, family, etc., make a game out of it. Whoever is last to the call has to answer a question in front of the group. Pick from the questions included in this book. Keep it fun and light and always be sensitive that there may have been a good reason the person was late!

Virtual Rock Paper Scissors

Time: 10 Minutes (or less)
Group: Up to 15
Logistics & Supplies: Video on
None

Rock, Paper, Scissors... Shoot! With cameras on, play a quick game of rock paper scissors for laughs, or as a fun way to decide who speaks next or takes on a disputed task! It's simple, the activity facilitator picks two people and together they say, "Rock, Paper, Scissors, Shoot!" As they say "Shoot", they hold up their hand to the camera with their move! Simple, quick and fun!

Reminder:
Rock – Hand in a fist
Scissors – Two fingers out (A Peace Sign sideways)
Paper – Flat hand

Rules
Rock beats Scissors
Scissors beats Paper
Paper beats Rock

Tip: Organize a team competition with brackets! John plays Kim, Pooja plays Ali, the winners of both play a best out of three game to win the team championship! Hype up the game with a little Rocky theme song playing in the background!

Two Truths and a Lie

Time: 10 Minutes (or less)
Group: Up to 15
Logistics & Supplies: None

This quick activity is simple: Have each person think of two interesting truths about themselves and one unassuming lie. Have one person start by sharing their three things: "I once met Bono from U2, I was fired from two jobs, and I am terrified of spiders." After they share, have others on the team try and guess which of the three things is a lie! (I am not scared of spiders!) After, people will often want to ask questions about the two truths, jumpstarting the group into a conversation!

Tip: Break up one of your meetings by having one person share their TT&L. If you want more people to participate, break people into pairs or small groups and do the activity with each other in breakout rooms!

Orchestra

Time: 10 Minutes (or less)
Group: Up to 15
Logistics & Supplies: Video on
                         None

Have everyone make one sound at a time. One person starts, then another, until everyone is making a sound in rhythm... or chaos. Either way, it should bring a few laughs! Try it a few times and see if you ever reach a bit of harmony!

Name that Tune

Time: 10 Minutes (or less)
Group: Up to 15
Logistics & Supplies: None

Start your team meeting with a little music and competition with a game of Name that Tune! Have everyone open up their group chat window, play the first 3-5 seconds of a song, the first person to type the name of the song wins! Rotate each meeting so everyone brings their own song.

Tip: Pick a theme like 80's or 90's, or pick an Artist/Genre based on the general music tastes of your team.
After, make a team playlist of all the songs.

Dress Up Day

Time: 10 Minutes (or less)
Group: No limit
Logistics & Supplies: Video on
Email instructions ahead of activity

Sunglasses Day, Fancy Hat Day, Black Tie Day, Band T-shirt Day, Virtual Mullet Day, the possibilities are endless! Bring out a few laughs by picking a fun dress code for your next meeting.

Tip: Surprise your team by randomly showing up to a video call in costume!

Charades

Time: 10 Minutes (or less)
Group: Up to 15/Teams
Logistics & Supplies: Charade prompts

This age-old rainy-day game is easy to play with virtual teams. With cameras on, divide your group into two teams, then explain the rules below.

Rules: One person from each team is going to be given a prompt via a private chat from the activity organizer. Without talking, using only your body and facial expression, you need to act out the word, phrase, or person you have been assigned. As the person acts out their prompt, the team members try to guess until they get it or until the 1-minute timer runs out. If a team member guesses the assigned word, phrase, or person correctly they get one point. After one team goes, the activity organizer sends a prompt to the other team and they repeat the activity. The team with the most points at the end wins!

Virtual Themed Bingo

Time: 10 Minutes (or less)
Group: Unlimited
Logistics & Supplies: Email Bingo cards ahead of time

Making your own custom version of bingo is much easier than you think. There are several sites online (example: *myfreebingocards. com*) that help automatically create cards that you can use in your next meeting. Take 5 minutes to develop your own cards, download them, send a card to each team member prior to your meeting, and you're ready to play!

Tip: Create a game around a current project or theme you have recently talked about.

Tip: Get people laughing by using different employee or customer names.

Tip: Make distributing the cards easy. After you make all the cards in one document, add numbers to each card. Then send the whole document to your team and just using a card number for each person. Work smart not hard!

Bingo Card Generator:
https://myfreebingocards.com/bingo-card-generator

Awkward Family Photo

Time: 10 Minutes (or less)
Group: Unlimited
Logistics & Supplies: Email instructions ahead of activity

Invite your people to share their best awkward photo with the group. Sweeten up the deal by offering an award (like lunch to the winner) as a prize for best photo! If you need additional ideas and laughs, check out the site awkwardfamilyphotos.com.

Team Mad Libs

Time: 10 Minutes (or less)
Group: Up to 15
Logistics & Supplies: Create team Mad Libs

If you have not heard of Mad Libs before, they are a sort of template story game, where people fill in blank spaces to create an often hilarious result. "When I heard our team would be working from home, I <Adverb> knew I wouldn't have nearly enough <Noun> to <Verb> for a month!" Create your own virtual team Mad Lib. Fill it in together on a call: "Folks, I have a Mad Lib story about working from home. John, give me an adverb, Maria give me a noun, and Phil give me a verb!" After the story is filled in, read back to your team for a few laughs!

Cracker Whistle

Time: 10 Minutes (or less)

Group: Up to 15

Logistics & Supplies: Ask people ahead of time to bring crackers to the call.

Have everyone show up to the call with a pack of dry crackers (Saltines, Soda Crackers, etc.) and something to cover their keyboard! One at a time, have people try and put two crackers in their mouth and whistle a tune of your choosing (Star Wars Theme, Baby Shark, etc.). Watch people laugh as the crackers come flying out of their mouth.

Ways to Learn & Grow Together

Epic Virtual Scavenger Hunt

Time: 30 Minutes—1 Hour
Group: Up to 15 /Teams
Logistics & Supplies
Preparation - Create virtual scavenger hunt questions
Divide participants into teams of 2-5 people.

In your next meeting, send your virtual team on a dynamic scavenger hunt! Here are a few ideas to get you thinking.

Google Maps Questions: You can visit basically anywhere in the world with Google Maps! Make up your own questions by picking a random place on the map, going to street view, and creating a question.

Example:

- Question: What is the name of the bar next to 377 Fore St Portland, ME 04101, USA?

Online Search Questions: Create your own questions

- What is the name of the famous hotel that was destroyed in the civil war in Beirut but is still standing empty today?
- Where is the original Hotel California from the Eagles song located?

Phone Call/Email Tasks:

- Call the Sunrise Diner in Kittery, Maine, and find out what the special is today and how much it costs. (Use people and places you know so you can call them ahead and let them know people will be calling.)

- Call Kim in HR and ask her what she thinks makes a great employee. Also, find out her favorite treat!

Find Things:
Whether they are at home or in the office, have people find random physical objects they then need to show you over video!
- Piece of cheese
- Bottle of wine
- Car Key
- Baby Picture
- Etc.

Tip: Use a platform like Zoom that allows you to put your teams in breakout rooms. This way, they can work through the questions as a team. As a facilitator, give the instructions as a whole group and then send people into breakout rooms. Bring them back from time to time to check on progress. After the activity, check people's answers as a group and have them debrief how it went. Note: While they are working, move from group to group to see how they are working together.

Houston (I Have Problem!) Brainstorm Sessions

Time: 30 Minutes—1 Hour

Group: Up to 6

Logistics & Supplies: Organizer prepares situation brief & invites 3-6 team members to join

Based on the famous line from the Apollo 13 space mission, where a team on the ground had to act fast to come up with a solution that saved their comrades up in space. When needed, employees can request a Houston Session. The purpose of the session is to use the combined wisdom of the group to get unstuck or generate creative solutions to a problem. The person in need invites a group of people to a session. Prior, they prepare a brief with the following information: the details of the problem, what they have already tried, and their current ideas. After the briefing, the participants ask questions and share their ideas and potential solutions.

Difficult Customer Role Play

Time: 30 Minutes

Group: Up to 15

Logistics & Supplies: Preparation - Collect difficult customer scenarios

Have every team member write a difficult customer scenario they have personally faced or they witnessed another team member face. Have people send their scenarios to the person who will act as the facilitator. Once all the scenarios are collected, have your team convene online. Next, have the facilitator send a scenario to someone who will act as the customer and assign another person the customer service representative role. Give them five minutes to act out the scenario on the call, and after, debrief as a team. If you have time, run through another situation.

Know Your Customers Activity

Time: 1 Hour+

Group: Up to 15

Logistics & Supplies: Preparation – Ask team members to interview 3-5 customers prior to your next meeting

Few things help us improve our product or services like taking time to understand the user experiences. Invite a client or customer to join one of your virtual meetings or send your people out to interview a few clients, then report what they learned.

Create a basic interview script and series of standard questions for people to use.

Sample Invite:

Dear ___, it's _____ from _____.

I hope this message finds you doing well. How is the team/family doing? My team and I are always looking for ways to better support the people we serve. This week and next, everyone on our team will be interviewing two clients and if you would be open, I would love the opportunity to interview you. I know you're busy, but if you could spare a quick 15 minutes, I would love to hear your input to better understand your experiences with our service. If you do not have time, I completely understand. Let me know if you would be open for a quick call.

Sincerely,

Sample Intro on Call

Hi _____ , it's _____ from _____.

Thank you for agreeing to have a quick call with me today. How have you been? As I mentioned in the email, the purpose of the call is to learn about your experience. Do you mind answering a few questions?

Possible Questions

- Why did you first choose to engage with our services?
- What has kept you with us?
- Has there ever been a time when you considered leaving? If so why, and why didn't you?
- What is your favorite part about working with us?
- What do you think we could do to take your experience to the next level?
- Anything else?

Online Customer/Employee Journey Mapping

Time: 1 Hour

Group: Up to 15

Logistics & Supplies: Preparation – Send the assignment to your team members to complete.

Invite your people to map out your online customer experience.

Assignment:

Before our next meeting, I would like everyone to pretend that you're a customer exploring our product/services (or employee considering working for us). I want you to go online and search for our company, then visit our site or other sites that talk about our products. What do you notice? What do you think first time customers see or notice? Take a few screen shots and come to our next meeting ready to discuss. Try to come up with one simple thing we could do to improve the online experience.

In your next meeting, ask everyone briefly to share about what they observed, their ideas for improvement, and if it would make a difference. Commit to follow up actions.

Children's Book Challenge

Time: 1 Hour+

Group: Up to 15

Logistics & Supplies: Peparation – Pick an activity prompt for your team

Break your people into two or three teams, depending on the size of your group (ideal team size is 3-5 people.) Task each team with creating a simple children's book to explain something about your work. Let them know that the purpose of the activity is to practice developing creative ways to simplify the complicated.

Example:

Life Insurance: Explain why life insurance is important to a 5-year-old.

Manufacturing: Explain how manufacturing works to a 5-year-old.

Software: Explain what our product does to a 5-year-old.

Rules:

Your book can be no longer than 15 pages (including a cover with the authors' names).

The final product should be delivered in a PDF or PPT.

Everyone on your team must contribute.

Select one person to read the story to the group (or have the authors rotate reading pages).

Don't worry about the final product being perfect, just get it done!

Set a time limit: Give people 1 hour to do the activity. Alternatively, explain the task to the team ahead of time and have them complete the challenge between meetings.

Debrief:
What did you learn from this activity?
How did your team develop and implement the ideas?
What from this activity can we bring back to our work?

Using the same basic structure as the children's book challenge, below are three additional team challenge ideas.

Facebook Challenge

(Use the same basic time and direction as the children's book challenge)

Break your group into two teams to create a new Facebook group or page. Have them create the header, footer, values statement, and even invite people to join. Prize goes to the team with the best page and most followers in the allotted time.

Billboard Challenge

(Use the same basic time and direction as the children's book challenge)

Break your people into teams and have everyone create a unique billboard to represent a message or motto for your product, mission, or company. Award points to the best design.

Commercial Challenge

(Use the same basic time and direction as the children's book challenge)

Have your remote people break into two teams and give them 1 hour to create a commercial for a new product or service. Have them come back and either play or present their commercial.

TED Talk Tuesdays

Time: 25-30 Minutes

Group: Unlimited

Logistics & Supplies: Select a TED Talk Discussion questions

There are thousands of amazing and free 5-20 minute TED talks online. Each week, invite people to have their lunch break in the conference room to watch a TED talk together, followed by a discussion.

Possible Questions:
- What resonated most with you about the talk?
- How do you feel this applies to you and/or the people you work with?
- What is one way you could apply this to your team?
- Below you will find the title of my TEDx talk and a few of my personal favorites! Do a quick search for the titles online and you will find them in seconds.

Christopher Littlefield: What do you want to be acknowledged for?

The human relationship to recognition, ineffective practices, and what makes a powerful thank you.

Simon Sinek: How great leaders inspire action

Inspiring video that talks about the importance of identifying our "Why!"

Dan Pink: The puzzle of motivation
Funny video that makes a research-based argument that incentives may kill performance.

Shawn Achor: The happiest secret to better work
Hilarious video talks about positive psychology at work and the role of happiness in performance.

Take a Course Together

Time: Based on Course
Group: Unlimited
Logistics & Supplies: Select a course to take as a team

Platforms like EdX, Coursera, and several others offer free online courses led by top professors around the world across all disciplines. Most courses are free, with an option to pay if you want a certificate of completion. Take a course on your own or take one as a team or office. Meet each week online to watch the videos and have discussions. Learn from the best for free! I recommend taking The Foundations of Happiness at Work with UC Berkeley Professor, Dacher Keltner.

Tip: Does your organization have an online learning platform? Support people in using it by organizing a time to take a course together.

Links:
www.coursera.org
www.edx.org
www.edx.org/course/the-foundations-of-happiness-at-work

Public Speaking Practice

Time: 30 Min – 1 Hour/Ongoing
Group: Up to 6
Logistics & Supplies: Video on

Support each other to develop your virtual and in-person presentation skills by organizing an online clinic. If someone has a presentation coming up and needs to practice, great, but if not, have everyone prepare a short 2-3 minute presentation on a topic of choice. After, have each person share feedback on what the presenter did well, and a few things they feel could take it to the next level.

Tip: Join or organize an Online Toastmasters Club at your organization. Go here for a list of online clubs. www.toastmasters. org/resources/online-only-clubs

Virtual Guest Speaker

Time: 30 Min—1 Hour
Group: Unlimited
Logistics & Supplies: Select and invite speaker

Mix up your meeting by inviting a guest speaker. Maybe a topic expert for your field, speaker on self-care, or even your HR partner to explain your new benefits package. Think about who you have in your personal network that your team could really learn from. Invite the person to join your next meeting.

Tip: Let people know ahead of time who will be joining and the structure of the talk: "I will give a two-minute intro, _____ speaker will talk for 15-20 minutes, and then we will open it up to questions. Please come with questions ready!"

Tip: Note many speakers, executive coaches, and health professionals are looking for opportunities to speak to organizations. When you see a speaker at a local event, invite them to join one of your virtual meetings. You may just be surprised if they say yes.

Invite the Boss

Time: 1 Hour
Group: Up to 20
Logistics & Supplies: Invite the boss
Ask employees to prepare questions

Give your people the opportunity to meet and learn from your organization's senior leadership. Ask your boss, supervisor, or even CEO if they would be willing to attend one of your virtual team meetings as a guest. Have your team prepare questions ahead of time and give them a chance to both share what they are working on and ask questions. This is not only a win for your people, but an opportunity to develop relationships with employees across the organization from the comfort of their office.

Tip: When you invite the leader, be clear about why you are inviting them and how they can help.

"My remote employees never get to connect with and meet senior leaders. I wanted to create an opportunity for them to meet you, share about their work, and be able to ask you a few questions. I know you are busy, but it would make a huge difference for the team if you could spare 20 minutes to connect with my remote team one day."

Cross Departmental Virtual Meet Up

Time: 1 Hour

Group: Up to 20

Logistics & Supplies: Invite another department
Ask employees to prepare questions/presentation
Cross Department Meeting questions

Sales, Marketing, IT, Finance, etc. Many times, different departments or divisions interact daily, but never really know each other. Organize a virtual meet up with another department. Give each team 5 minutes to provide an update on their current projects, objectives, and how other teams can best support them. Below are a few great questions:

Great Cross Department Meeting Questions
- How do you explain to friends what your department does?
- What is your team working on right now?
- What do you wish others understood about your role, department, and what it takes to do your job?
- How can we help make your job easier?
- What are the indicators our divisions are working well together?
- What are early warning signs we are not working as well as we could?
- What things can we do, that take under 10 minutes, that will help us keep working well together?

Tip: Can't get everyone together for a virtual meet up? Invite a few people from each team to connect. After, have them report back to the rest of the team.

Tip: Run the event like a virtual networking session. Pair people up and have them answer the questions above.

Facilitate a Virtual Networking Event

Time: 1 Hour/Ongoing
Group: Up to 15
Logistics & Supplies: Video on Preparation – send invitation

One of the challenges of working remotely is not having the opportunity to network with colleagues or others in your field when you live on the other side of the country or world. Help your remote employees meet others in your organization or field by organizing a virtual networking event. Invite a group of people you think should meet to a virtual happy hour or networking session. As the activity organizer, once people arrive, thank them for attending. If you know everyone, go around and give a quick intro and tell others who the people are and why you invited them. If you don't know people, have everyone go around and do a quick intro. Ask people to answer the below information about themselves in a minute or less. Next, inform people you will split them up into breakout rooms for the next five minutes and then rotate people for a new networking session.

After, bring everyone back together, thank them for their attendance, and ask if they are interested in doing something like this in the future!

Introduction Information
- Name
- Location
- Organization/Field
- One thing they are passionate about right now

How many people:

- Invite 6-8 people max

Who to Invite:

People from your team

Other departments

Friend you met at a conference or went to university with

Pick people you would love to be stuck talking with

Provide people with a few questions to ask if needed.

Virtual Book/Movie Club

Time: 1 Hour/Ongoing
Group: Up to 15
Logistics & Supplies: Introduce book/movie and invite
members to join

Organize a virtual book club with your team, group of coworkers, or friends. Just as if you were in the same location as the group, pick a book or article to read and invite people to a virtual meet up to discuss and reflect. If you are a leader, maybe buy a digital copy of the book or article for your team and then schedule a meeting for people to come together to reflect on the book.

Movie Club: Are people on your team not into reading? Try a movie club or podcast club instead!

Virtual Lunch & Learn

Time: 30 Min—1-Hour
Group: Up to 15
Logistics & Supplies: Video on
Organize first presentation and guests

Julie consistently gets the highest customer rating, Maria is a master of Excel, Kim is a CrossFit fanatic, Matt is an International Biscuit Baking champion. You have a wealth of knowledge and expertise on your team, use it! Invite staff members to run a mini virtual training session for their peers. Ask Julie if she would be open to hosting a mini training session and sharing her philosophy and process in working with customers. Not only do people get to learn from one another, but you acknowledge the person by giving them an opportunity to share their passion and success. (Tip: After each training, ask who else would like to run a mini training session or who they would like to learn from on the team or in the organization. Before you leave, schedule the next mini program.)

Tip: Invite people from other teams, departments, and even companies to join!

Trivia Time

Time: 10 Minutes (or less)
Group: Teams 3-4 people
Logistics & Supplies: Select trivia questions

Infuse a little playful rivalry by organizing a trivia competition. You can either make this a one-off event during a meeting, or an ongoing competition where you ask one question at the start or end of each call. Either way, divide your people into two to three teams and let the competition begin. Make up your own question or do a quick search for "trivia questions" and you will have thousands to choose from. Sweeten the deal by having a prize for the winner!

Team Photo Competition

Time: 10 Minutes (or less)
Group: Unlimited
Logistics & Supplies: Send photo prompt

Support your people in their creative side by hosting a team photo competition. In the beginning of the week, send out a prompt (see below for ideas), and have everyone submit a photo by the end of the week for the team to vote on!

Photo Prompts:
- Edible
- Round
- Small/Large
- Metal
- Reflection
- Self Portrait
- Out of Place

Tip: Do you work in a field like architecture, marketing, or life sciences? Create a prompt that has people shoot photos of things relevant to your subject area. Help your people keep looking for the beauty in their field.

Tip: Save all the photos and create an album or book for your staff at the end of the year as a gift!

Ways to Stay Healthy as a Team

Two Minute Mindful Meeting Transition

Time: 2 Minutes
Group: Unlimited
Logistics & Supplies: None

Often, people show up on a call and the meeting begins with half the group still trying to process the previous meeting/task they just came from. Try starting your next meeting with a Two-Minute Mindful Transition. Once people join the meeting, say *"Let's take a few minutes to transition into our meeting."*

Steps:

First, give people a minute to note any thoughts or follow up actions from their previous meeting, so they can be present in the current meeting.

Second, ask people to put everything down, then take 3-5 deep breaths together.

Third, welcome people to the meeting and begin.

Gratitude Journals

Time: 10 Minutes (or less)
Group: Up to 15
Logistics & Supplies: None

Research has found that people who take 5-10 minutes at the beginning or end of their day to write down 3-5 things they are grateful for or proud of, are 100% happier, healthier, and even lose weight! Why? What we focus on is what we get. If we take time to see the good, we tend to see ourselves and the world around us in a better light! Start a team gratitude practice by starting or finishing your call or virtual meeting by having everyone writing down 3-5 things for which they are grateful. After, ask if anyone wants to share the things they wrote down. If your team communicates via chat, post the question in your group every Monday and every Friday. As facilitator, post your three things to help jumpstart people sharing.

Try taking it on for 21 days and see how it impacts you and your team members lives.

Thankful-Thursday & 22 Gratitude Prompts

Time: 10 Minutes (or less)
Group: Up to 15
Logistics & Supplies: None

Initiate a team gratitude practice by starting a "What's Good Wednesday "or "Thankful Thursday." Each week, post a question via email or Slack and invite your teammates to reflect. Answer the question yourself first to help encourage others to do the same. Below are 22 questions to help get you started:

Trigger Gratitude (22 Questions)

1. Who are the people I am grateful for in my life right now and why?

2. What has happened in the last week that I am grateful for?

3. What small pleasure do I experience each day, but do so without thinking?

4. What experiences have I had recently that I appreciate?

5. What have I gotten to learn recently that has helped me grow?

6. What opportunities do I currently have that I am grateful for?

7. What physical abilities do I have but take for granted?

8. What material possessions am I grateful for having and why?

9. What did I see today or over the last month that was beautiful?

10. Who at work am I happy to see each day and why?

11. Who is someone on my team I am grateful I get to work with and why?

12. Who is someone on another team I am grateful I get to work with and why?

13. What about my job am I grateful for and why?

14. What about my commute am I grateful for and why?

15. Who is a person that I don't speak to often, but, if I lost them tomorrow, it would be devastating? (Take this as a cue to reach out today!)

16. What am I better at today than I was a year ago?

17. Who is a person that challenges me to be better?

18. What opportunities do other people in my life have that I am grateful for?

19. What material object do I use every day that I am thankful for having?

20. What has someone done for me recently that I am grateful for?

21. Who do I not know personally, but I am grateful for?

22. What are the three things I am grateful for right now?

The questions above were originally published in my article in Harvard Business Review Ascend titled How to Trigger Gratitude in Ourselves and Others.[4]

---

4.   Christopher Littlefield, "How to Trigger Gratitude in Ourselves and Others," Ascend HBR, last modified November 26, 2019, https://hbrascend. org/topics/how-to-trigger-gratitude-in-ourselves-and-others/.

Do a Health Challenge Together as a Team

Time: Based on the activity
Group: Unlimited
Logistics & Supplies: Dependent upon the activity

Just because you're not in the same location does not mean you can't share activities together. Here are a few ideas:

Run A Race Together
Have everyone sign up for a 5K or half marathon around the same time. Support each other in your training and have people post their runs in your daily chats. Add a little purpose and maybe turn your training into a fundraiser.

Participate in a group health challenge that you can do from anywhere.
Check out programs like Global Challenge and Whole Life Challenge where you and your team can have fun and develop healthy habits in the process.

Global Challenge: Health Wellness Activity
https://globalchallenge.virginpulse.com

Whole Life Challenge: 8 Week Health and Wellbeing Challenge
https://www.wholelifechallenge.com

Walking Virtual Meetings

Whether it's a one on one or team meeting, invite people to go for a walk or be outdoors if it is nice for your meetings. When you take the action as a leader, you invite your people to do the same.

Stretch & Hydration Breaks

If your meetings regularly go over 40 minutes, set a timer and take a five-minute break to stretch and hydrate.

Virtual Yoga Class

Do you have a yoga instructor or other fitness instructor on your team? Invite them to teach a class for the group. If not, maybe find a Video online and do a class together.

Celebration & Recognition

Shout Outs

Time: 10 Minutes (or less)
Group: Up to 15
Logistics & Supplies: None

Carve out time in each one of your weekly or biweekly meetings for shout outs. At the start or end of your call, ask if anyone wants to make a shout out to anyone on your team or on another team.

"I want to give a shout out to Phil who really helped me last week with my presentation. I asked him for feedback and he picked up on two major errors and showed me how to make one of my slides much easier to understand – it made a huge difference!"

Tip: Make it a ritual. Ask the same question at the start or end of each meeting and your people will start going prepared to share.

Small Victories

Time: 10 Minutes (or less)
Group: Up to 15
Logistics & Supplies: None

Help your people step away from their never-ending to-do list and get present to what they are accomplishing each week with a "Small Victories or Weekly Wins" practice. Every Thursday, make a quick post to your team chat or Facebook group for everyone to share at least one "Small Victory." Maybe you called a client you have been avoiding, finished a report, onboarded a new team member, submitted your taxes, or went for a run! It can be work or personal, but the point is to create a space where people get present and feel safe to share their progress!

Work Anniversary/Birthday Compliment List

Time: 10 Minutes (or less) + Prep
Group: Up to 15
Logistics & Supplies: Preparation – Create quick survey & email

Give people an opportunity to express their appreciation and admiration for their coworker with a virtual compliment list. This is a great way to celebrate an individual's birthday, work anniversary, or retirement! Create a simple online form using something like Survey Monkey or Typeform. Create a survey for the person whose birthday it is, send it out to coworkers, supervisors, clients, and family members, if you have their emails, and ask them to fill it out. After, compile the responses into a framed photo, PowerPoint, card, or have someone in the same location post the comments around their office or house!

Intro:
Hello everyone, as many of you know next week is Maria's (Birthday, Work Anniversary, Retirement). Help me make that day special by taking a minute to let her know what you appreciate or admire about her. Attached is a link to an online form. Please take five minutes to fill it out. After, I will take all the responses and compile them into something special for her!

Tip: Run this as a team activity. Create one form but make a text box for everyone on your team. Send it out to everyone and ask them to take a few minutes to write a quick note of appreciation or admiration to their coworkers. Let people know they can leave their compliment anonymously or in their name. After, print out the lists and send them to everyone to read and enjoy.

Unforgettable Thank You Video

Time: 1-2 Hours

Group: Unlimited

Logistics & Supplies: Preparation – Send invite for people to record and share a video message. Combine the videos into a video presentation.

Give someone a gift they will never forget by making them a thank you video. Whether it's a work anniversary, birthday, or retirement, ask coworkers, clients, friends, and family to record a quick 15-20 second message. Drop all the videos together into a quick video, add a song, and surprise them with it at your next meeting. I guarantee they will never forget it!

Virtual Birthday Party

Time: 1-Hour
Group: Up to 15
Logistics & Supplies: Preparation

Just because a team member is not in your office, does not mean you can't get them a cake and celebrate their birthday! Surprise your employee by finding a local bakery that delivers or messaging their family member and asking them to pick one up and hide it in the fridge. If all else fails, order Tastykakes or Hostess cakes and a pack of candles and send it to them! Invite the team together and sing Happy Birthday!

Appreciation Prompts

Time: 10 Minutes (or less)
Group: Up to 15
Logistics & Supplies: None

Today, nudge your team to take 5-minutes to express their appreciation for the people around them. Cut and paste one of the prompts below into your team's chat to get the conversation going.

- Today, thank a person in IT, HR, Maintenance, or Accounting.
- Today, thank someone at work who inspires you.
- Today, thank a client or customer that you really enjoy working with.
- Today, thank someone on your team who flies under the radar, but always gets the job done.
- Today, thank someone who is going through some tough times (divorce, health/financial issues, problems with their parents/kids) and still shows up each day.
- Today, thank someone who has taken on a new role or task recently and really stepped up to the occasion.
- Today, thank someone who always finds a way to show up on time.
- Today, thank someone who took feedback to heart and really took on improving their performance.
- Today, thank someone who has been covering multiple roles/functions as people are out or positions are empty.
- Today, thank someone who brings fun and laughter to your day.

Virtual Hand-Written Thank You Note (Not an E-card!)

Time: 10 Minutes (or less)
Group: Up to 15
Logistics & Supplies: None

Just because you can't drop a hand-written thank you note on the desk of a coworker doesn't mean you need to revert to sending an impersonal e-card! The reason a hand-written card is often more meaningful for the recipient is the fact that the giver invested the time to write out their message and deliver it. If you want to make your message a little more meaningful than an email, invest five minutes to write your message on a card, a piece of paper, or even a sticky note. Take a photo of the card and send it to the person with a note, "Next time I see you, I will give you the hard copy... thank you!" Want to take it one step further? Record your thank you message in a video and send it to them. Regardless, if you send a photo of your card or a video message, you are guaranteed to make their day!

Not sure what to say? Here are a few ideas to get you started.

- Thank you for coming in early every day.
- Thank you for taking on the last-minute project last week.
- Thank you for being one of the people who always stays to help clean up after events.
- Thank you for being a sounding board for my ideas.
- Thank you for always taking time to make sure I take care of myself.
- Thank you for always asking about my kids.
- Thank you for being the person who always make people smile.

- Thank you for your creativity.
- Thank you for always challenging my ideas.
- Thank you for always labeling files in a way we can actually find them on the shared server.
- Thank you for always remembering people's birthdays.
- Thank you for always getting everyone's paycheck out on time.
- Thank you for always coming prepared to meetings.
- Thank you for always asking me if I want coffee when you go to Starbucks.
- Thank you for always sharing interesting articles and events.
- Thank you for reminding me to go home at night.
- Thank you for always inviting me to events even if I don't go.
- Thank you for always getting your work done on time
- Thank you for always reminding us we could collaborate with other departments.
- Thank you for putting up with my craziness.
- Thank you for answering the same question multiple times when I get overworked.
- Thank you for always pushing for us to try new things.
- Thank you for always keeping our people safe.
- Thank you for always keeping our computer working 364 days a year.
- Thank you for stepping up and covering the extra workload when a team member was out.
- Thank you for always telling me when I have food in my teeth when no one else does.
- Thank you for being you.
- Thank you for making me laugh.

Additional Simple Actions & Ideas
to Support Your People Virtually

Stay Connected and Have Fun
- Organize a 15-minute virtual coffee break each day.
- If you use Slack or another internal chat program, create a channel for Kitten videos, Riddles, and Motivational quotes
- Organize a virtual Happy Hour
- Host a virtual Cooking Class
- Play online games like Words with Friends or Scrabble together
- Watch a movie together with Netflix Party

Engage with People's Families
- Organize an Art Contest for employees' kids.
- Organize a Virtual Trivia Night and invite people's families to attend.
- Create virtual networking groups like "Parents in Quarantine" "Spouses networking group"
- After a busy period, send thank you notes to the families of your employees for supporting them during the busy times.

Support People's Growth
- Cross train people in different functions.
- Share learning opportunities, courses, and workshops you think they may find interesting.
- Invite people to attend senior meetings, if appropriate.
- Use your network to pair people with mentors in the roles or fields they want to work in.
- Create a position or opportunity for them to develop the skills they want to learn.
- Do they want to develop their public speaking? Assign them to present at your next all staff meeting and hire a speaking coach to help them prepare.

- Support someone to attend a conference in their area.
- Do you offer tuition reimbursement or flexible schedule at work? Support people to grow outside of work by getting a degree.

Bibliography

Beck, Randall, and Jim Harter. "Managers Account for 70% of Variance in Employee Engagement." Gallup - Business Journal. Last modified April 21, 2015. https://news.gallup.com/ businessjournal/182792/managers-account-variance-employee-engagement.aspx.

Dethmer, Jim, Diana Chapman, and Kaley Klemp. *The 15 commitments of conscious leadership: a new paradigm for sustainable success*. United States: Conscious Leadership Group, 2015.

Grenny, Joseph. "How to Raise Sensitive Issues During a Virtual Meeting." Harvard Business Review. Last modified March 14, 2017. https://hbr.org/2017/03/how-to-raise-sensitive-issues-during-a-virtual-meeting.

Littlefield, Christopher. "How to Trigger Gratitude in Ourselves and Others." Ascend HBR. Last modified November 26, 2019. https://hbrascend.org/topics/how-to-trigger-gratitude-in-ourselves-and-others/.

About the Author

 Christopher Littlefield is an International/ TEDx Speaker, Forbes and Harvard Business Review Contributor, and founder of Beyond Thank You. As an expert in employee appreciation, recognition and workplace culture, he has trained thousands of leaders across six continents at organizations like Accenture, Boston Medical, Salesforce, Reserve Bank of Australia, U.S. Army, United Nations, and more. Learn more about Christopher Littlefield at beyondthankyou.com

Made in United States
North Haven, CT
06 June 2022

19927344R00075